This book belongs to:

_____

_____

To my firstborn Sara for inspiring me
- M. M.

Published by Mona Mustafa
Calgary, Alberta, Canada
www.monamustafa.com
Instagram:@monamustafa89

Text copyright © 2024 by Mona Mustafa
Illustrations copyright © 2024 Mona Mustafa
Book Illustration and Design: Abeer Jakmiri
Edited by: Naima B. Robert

All rights reserved. No part of this publication may be reproduced, stored in a retrieval system, or transmitted in any way or by any means, electronic, mechanical, photo copying, recording, or otherwise, without the prior written permission of the publisher.

ISBN: 978-1-7380386-0-2

START WITH BISMILLAH

Written by: Mona Mustafa
Illustrated by: Abeer Jakmiri

Finally, it was the big day, the day of the Quran competition at the masjid in the center of Istanbul. Sara spent the whole week revising Juz Amma with her family, like all the other seven-year-olds in her neighbourhood.

On Monday, She and Mama listened to Surah Al-Kafirun while having lunch. "Bismillah," Sara said as she took the first bite of her falafel wrap.

On Tuesday, Sara prayed Isha with her parents, and her father recited Surah Al-Fil. "Bismillah…" he said as he started. "I know this one," she thought gleefully, as she quietly recited along.

On Wednesday, Jidda came for dinner. "Sara, would you read Surah An-Nas for me?" Sara sat in Jidda's lap and recited An-Nas. "Bismillah…" she said as she began.

On 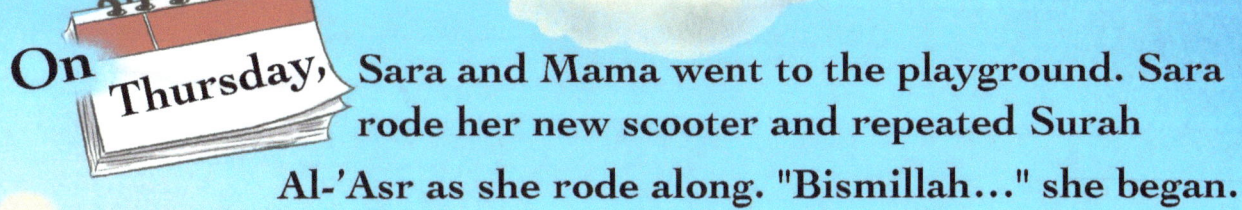 Sara and Mama went to the playground. Sara rode her new scooter and repeated Surah Al-'Asr as she rode along. "Bismillah…" she began.

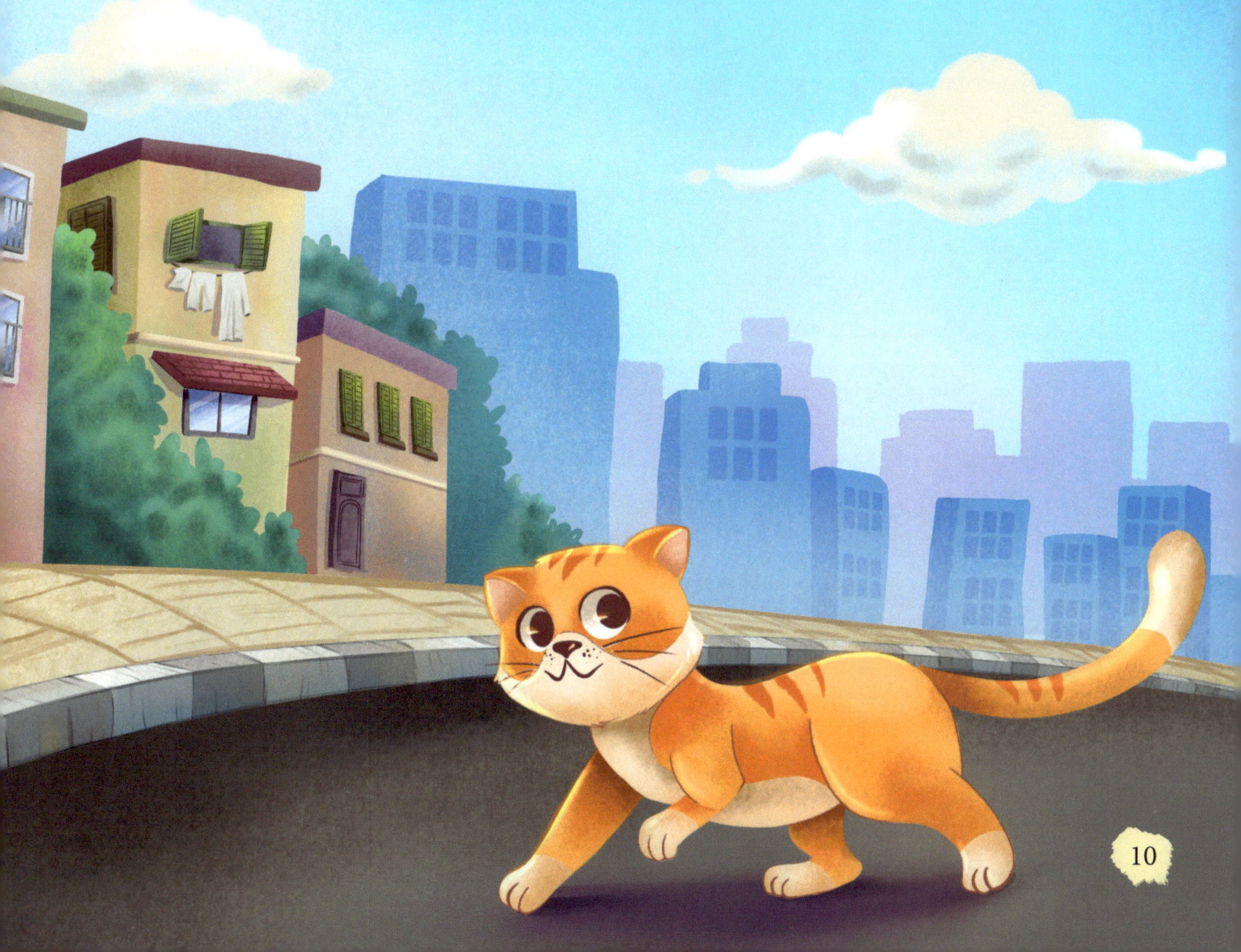

On the way back, it suddenly started to rain, a cold spring rain. Mama and Sara got wet as they hurried home. Later that night, Sara fell ill.

"Ahem, ahem. Bismillah," she tried to clear her throat over and over again, but her attempts were all in vain.

"Mama, what am I going to do tomorrow? How am I going to recite?!" she asked, her voice cracking. Mama gave her a warm cup of ginger lemon tea.

"Say 'Bismillah,' it will cure you and bring goodness and Barakah your way," said Mama. "Bismillah," said Sara as she drank.

Sara was exhausted from the long and tiring day, so Mama tucked her in bed and gave her a kiss on her warm forehead.

When she woke up the next morning, her voice was still hoarse, and her throat a little itchy.

But Sara felt well-rested and was ready for her breakfast.
"But first a spoonful of honey," said Mama. "Bismillah,"

After breakfast, Sara put on her jacket and shoes and went to the door where her parents were waiting. "You did your very best, and Allah will take care of the rest," said Baba as they all left for the contest.

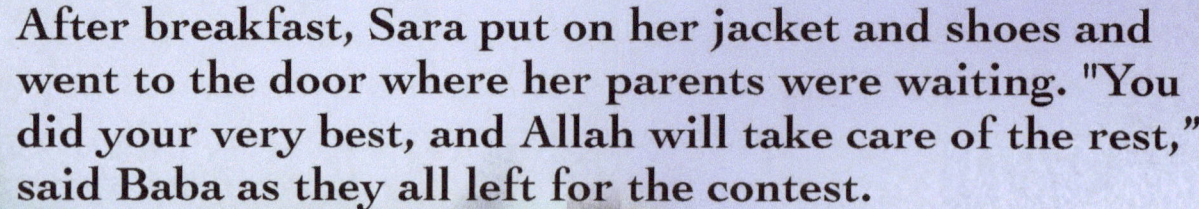

She took a deep breath and listened to the other children reciting. She closed her eyes and tried to recall the verses of Surah Al-Kawthar.

She cleared her throat once, twice, three times. Then she heard her name, and her heart started to pound so loudly she thought everyone could hear it.

Sara lifted her head up, collected all the courage she had, and sat in front of a Sheikh with a grey beard. "He looks just like my Jiddu," she thought to herself. Then "Bismillah…," Sara recited Surah Al-Humazah.

The Sheikh nodded his head with approval. "Mashallah! Well done, Sara," he said. Mama stood up and rushed to give Sara hugs and kisses. "I am so proud of you!" she said.

On the way home, Sara asked, "Mama, how did I manage to recite so well, after being sick and nervous?"

Mama replied, "Bismillah brings blessings, goodness, and ease. When you say Bismillah, you are asking Allah for help to cure you when you are sick and to ease your difficulties when in hardship. Do you understand, my darling girl?"

Sara smiled and nodded. She understood perfectly, Alhamdulillah. Bismillah made all the difference.

Glossary

Baba (BAH-bah) - father

Barakah (bah-RAH-kah) - blessing

Jiddu (JID-doo) - grandfather

Jidda (JID-duh) - grandmother

Mama (MAH-mah) - mother

Sheikh (SHEE-KH) - an elder

© 2024 Mona Mustafa . "All Rights Reserved"

www.ingramcontent.com/pod-product-compliance
Lightning Source LLC
Chambersburg PA
CBHW042250100526
44587CB00002B/90